DELIVER ME FROM NOWHERE:

The Untold Journey Behind Springsteen's Most Honest Album

STAN H. DANIEL

Copyright Page

All rights reserved. No part of this publication may be reproduced, distributed, or transmitted in any form or by any means, including photocopying, recording, or other electronic or mechanical methods, without the prior written permission of the author, except in the case of brief quotations embodied in critical reviews and certain other noncommercial uses permitted by copyright law.

Copyright © 2025 by Stan H. Daniel

Gratitude

This book would not have been possible without the creative spirit and enduring legacy of Bruce Springsteen. His willingness to lay bare the human condition—through raw lyrics, quiet moments, and unflinching honesty—inspired every page of this work. Nebraska wasn't just an album; it was a revelation. And for that, I'm deeply thankful.

To Warren Zanes, whose book Deliver Me from Nowhere offered such a thoughtful and intimate look into Springsteen's process—thank you for illuminating the corners where most biographies rarely shine.

I'm also grateful to the filmmakers, cast, and crew behind Springsteen: Deliver Me from Nowhere for bringing this powerful chapter of Bruce's life to the screen with care and sincerity. Jeremy Allen White's performance especially deserves recognition for its emotional restraint and truthfulness.

To the readers, fans, and fellow believers in music that moves the soul—thank you for picking up this book. Whether you're here as a lifelong fan or just discovering Springsteen's quieter side, your time and attention mean everything.

And finally, to the quiet spaces, the late-night headphones, the empty roads, and all the moments in between—thank you for making room for Nebraska.

Disclaimer

This book is an independent work of commentary, analysis, and appreciation. It is not authorized, endorsed, or affiliated with Bruce Springsteen, his management, Columbia Records, 20th Century Studios, Scott Cooper, Warren Zanes, or any individuals or entities associated with the making of the album Nebraska or the film Deliver Me from Nowhere.

All names, trademarks, and copyrights mentioned in this book are the property of their respective owners and are used here solely for the purposes of commentary, review, and analysis, as permitted under the Fair Use doctrine.

While every effort has been made to ensure the accuracy and reliability of the information presented, the author makes no warranties or representations and assumes no legal liability or responsibility for errors, omissions, or outcomes resulting from the use of this material.

This book is intended for informational and educational purposes only. The views and opinions expressed herein are those of the author and do not necessarily reflect the official policies or positions of any other individual, company, or organization.

TABLE OF CONTENTS

INTRODUCTION

Chapter 1: The Boy from Freehold
A Working-Class Start
The Soundtrack of a Small Town

Chapter 2: Hungry Heart, Restless Soul
Becoming The Boss
Fame, Pressure, and the Cost of Success

Chapter 3: Ghosts on the Highway
Bruce and the Burden of Expectation
The Road That Led to Nebraska

Chapter 4: The Nebraska Sessions
Four Tracks and a Bedroom
Why He Walked Away from the E Street Band (Temporarily)

Chapter 5: Stories in the Static
The Characters of Nebraska: Killers, Drifters, and Dreamers
Stark Honesty as a Creative Choice

Chapter 6: Reception and Reflection
Critics, Fans, and the Music Industry's Reaction
How Time Changed the Album's Legacy

Chapter 7: Deliver Me from Nowhere — Book to Screen
Warren Zanes and the Source Material
Adapting a Quiet Story for the Big Screen

Chapter 8: Casting the Legend
Jeremy Allen White as Bruce Springsteen
Portraying Real People with Weight and Accuracy

Chapter 9: Inside the Film
Scene by Scene: What the Film Shows
What It Leaves Out — and Why

Chapter 10: Direction and Style
Scott Cooper's Vision
Mood, Color, and Cinematic Silence

Chapter 11: The Sound of Nebraska Reimagined
Music Direction and Live Performances in the Film
Reinterpreting the Album for a New Audience

Chapter 12: Real vs. Represented
Where the Film Stays True
Creative Liberties and What They Mean

Chapter 13: Legacy and the Long View
Why Nebraska Still Matters
Springsteen's Continued Influence on Music and Film

INTRODUCTION

In the long and storied career of Bruce Springsteen, few moments feel as stark, haunting, or revealing as the creation of his 1982 album Nebraska. Stripped of the roaring anthems and stadium-born electricity of the E Street Band, Nebraska wasn't just a musical pivot—it was a confessional. A turning inward.

A deep breath taken in the middle of a storm. It was the sound of a man pulling back the curtain not only on America's forgotten corners but also on his own heart.

This book is about that moment.

It's about the real Bruce Springsteen—the man behind Born to Run and Darkness on the Edge of Town, yes—but more intimately, the man who recorded an entire album alone in a bedroom with a 4-track cassette recorder. It's about where he was emotionally, artistically, and spiritually during the making of Nebraska, and how the pain, pressure, and isolation of that era led to a piece of work that feels less like a commercial product and more like a diary never meant to be read.

It's also about how that quiet story, one that could've easily stayed buried beneath louder hits and bigger albums, is now being retold in a bold new way. Springsteen: Deliver Me from Nowhere, the film inspired by Warren Zanes' deeply personal book, brings that vulnerable moment back to life.

Directed by Scott Cooper and starring Jeremy Allen White as Springsteen, the film doesn't try to mythologize its subject. Instead, it leans into the silence. It lingers in the pauses, the blank pages, and the unlit corners of a superstar's psyche. It reminds us that even those we idolize carry shadows.

This introduction is your entry point into all of it—the music, the man, the movie.

A Legend Before the Silence

By the early 1980s, Bruce Springsteen was already a household name. His 1975 breakthrough album Born to Run catapulted him from local hero to national icon. By the time The River came out in 1980, he was selling out arenas and earning the kind of breathless media coverage reserved for rock legends.

The "working-class poet" image was set. So was the sound: loud, electric, full of life. A Bruce Springsteen album meant movement—both sonic and emotional.

But in the wake of all that success, something shifted.

Behind the scenes, Springsteen was grappling with deep-rooted insecurities, unresolved childhood trauma, and the psychological weight of fame. He later spoke openly about his battles with depression and the ways those internal struggles shaped his work. The Nebraska period, in particular, wasn't just a stylistic experiment. It was a lifeline.

When Springsteen sat down in his New Jersey home with nothing but a guitar, a harmonica, and a tape recorder, he wasn't trying to reinvent his career. He was trying to find his footing. What emerged was an album full of ghosts, criminals, fugitives, dreamers, and dead ends. Nebraska is bleak, yes—but never hollow. In its quietness, it speaks volumes.

Why Nebraska Still Matters

More than four decades after its release, Nebraska remains one of Springsteen's most revered and mysterious works. It's not an album designed for commercial success, and it never pretended to be. The songs are sparse.

The production is raw. And yet, it connects—perhaps more than any of his other records—with listeners who've felt alienated, unmoored, or misunderstood.

Why?

Because Nebraska strips away every layer of polish. There's no band to hide behind. No big solos. No arena choruses. Just Bruce, telling stories. Some are fictional, like the chilling title track inspired by real-life serial killer Charles Starkweather. Others feel semi-autobiographical—reflections of a man looking in the mirror and not entirely recognizing who he's become.

This vulnerability is what gives Nebraska its power. And it's what makes the story behind it worth telling again, this time through the lens of a film.

A Film That Whispers Instead of Shouts

When word got out that Nebraska would be the focus of a biopic, the reaction was mixed. Some cheered. Others worried. After all, how do you make a movie about an album that thrives on stillness?

But Scott Cooper, known for atmospheric, character-driven films like Crazy Heart and Hostiles, seemed like the right choice. He understood that this wasn't just a music movie. It was a portrait of a man on the edge of something—fame, breakdown, clarity—and the choice to center on this quieter chapter gave the film a refreshing purpose.

Jeremy Allen White, known for his role in The Bear, brings an introspective energy to Springsteen. He doesn't try to mimic every vocal inflection or facial tic. He plays Bruce from the inside out—subtle, thoughtful, sometimes volatile. He sings, too. And while no one can truly replicate the voice of Springsteen, White brings something honest to the performance: humility.

The film doesn't try to explain Nebraska in linear terms. It doesn't reduce Springsteen to bullet points or clichés. Instead, it walks alongside him, observing the silence, the breakdowns, the writing process, the detachment from the E Street Band. It shows a man withdrawing not to hide—but to listen. To himself. To his memories. To the sound of nothing, which became the sound of Nebraska.

From Book to Screen: Warren Zanes' Influence

Before the film, there was the book: Deliver Me from Nowhere by Warren Zanes. A musician and author himself, Zanes brought a personal, almost reverent lens to the subject. His interviews with Springsteen and his ability to weave emotion into facts made the book a unique entry into the Springsteen canon.

Zanes didn't just dissect the album. He tried to understand it—what it cost Bruce to make it, what it meant for his future, and why Nebraska continues to haunt listeners today. His work provided the emotional architecture on which the film is built.

And his title? A line from the song "State Trooper," one of the most haunting on the album: "Deliver me from nowhere."

That line became more than just a lyric. It became the thesis of an era.

A Story Worth Retelling

There are countless rock biopics out there. Most follow a similar path: humble beginnings, breakthrough, spiral, redemption. But Deliver Me from Nowhere is different because Nebraska is different. This isn't a story about excess or collapse. It's about quiet perseverance. It's about what happens when a man turns down the volume on the world and forces himself to sit with what's left.

In a time when louder often seems better—bigger tours, bolder branding, constant noise—this story reminds us that some of the most meaningful work happens in silence. Springsteen didn't need to shout to be heard. He just needed to be honest.

And that's what this book hopes to capture.

We'll begin by exploring Springsteen's early life and rise to fame, so we can better understand what led to this pivotal moment. Then we'll walk through the making of Nebraska, both technically and emotionally. From there, we'll dig into the legacy of the album, the making of the film, and how both versions—real and reimagined—continue to resonate.

This isn't just about one album or one movie. It's about what art can do when it stops performing and starts revealing. It's about finding meaning in the pauses.

And maybe, if we're lucky, it's about being delivered—from nowhere, to somewhere more human.

The Boy from Freehold

A Working-Class Start

Bruce Springsteen wasn't born on stage, guitar in hand, and wrapped in a flag. Before he became The Boss, before the sold-out arenas and presidential medals, he was just a boy from Freehold, New Jersey—a place where stories didn't make headlines and dreams were often traded for factory shifts.

Freehold was a working-class town in every sense of the word: modest homes, narrow streets, Catholic churches, and quiet resentment for anything that felt like it was out of reach. Born on September 23, 1949, to Douglas and Adele Springsteen, Bruce grew up in a home where money was tight and emotions often ran high. His father, Doug, struggled with employment and depression.

He worked sporadically as a bus driver and factory worker but battled inner demons that would later inspire some of Bruce's most powerful songs. Adele, his mother, worked as a legal secretary and held the family together with grit, grace, and a steady paycheck. Bruce would later credit her with being the first strong, steady force in his life.

The house they lived in was small, sometimes crumbling. The furniture was secondhand. They weren't poor in the sense of going without basic needs, but they weren't far from it either. Freehold was the kind of town where people didn't ask for much, and they didn't expect much in return. That quiet acceptance of limitation left an impression on Bruce.

He watched his father wrestle with invisible burdens and saw how the weight of unrealized dreams could wear a man down. These early experiences planted the seeds of restlessness, rebellion, and reflection that would later define his music. It was also a town full of contradictions. On one hand, it was tight-knit and familiar. On the other hand, it could feel like a trap.

As Bruce got older, he became increasingly aware of the unspoken social codes and the invisible walls that defined his world. His Catholic upbringing taught him about guilt and redemption, but it also stoked a fire in him to break out of every mold he was handed. Music became his escape. More than that, it became his map. He wasn't a sports kid, nor was he academically inclined.

What he had, early on, was an instinct—a pull toward sound, rhythm, and the stories buried in lyrics. He found his first love in rock and roll, the kind that pulsed through the radio like a promise. Elvis Presley lit the fuse. After seeing The King on "The Ed Sullivan Show," Bruce saw what was possible, and from that moment on, music wasn't just a dream. It was a direction.

The Soundtrack of a Small Town

The streets of Freehold didn't just raise Bruce; they echoed in his work. His earliest songs were filled with the texture of small-town life—working men clocking in at factories, lovers sneaking out in cars, and the inescapable sense that something bigger was always out of reach.

He saw the town not through rose-colored glasses but with a clarity that allowed him to capture its poetry and pain in equal measure. He started performing at local venues in his teens, eventually joining bands like The Castiles, Steel Mill, and Dr. Zoom & the Sonic Boom.

These early groups laid the groundwork for what would later become the E Street Band, but more importantly, they gave Bruce the freedom to experiment with sound and narrative. He wasn't just playing music; he was learning how to tell stories that mattered.

The physical setting of Freehold became a character in his songs, almost as if the streets, diners, and train tracks had voices of their own. In "My Hometown," Bruce captured the essence of that place: the pride, the decline, the nostalgia, and the unshakeable bond between a person and where they're from. The song is more than a recollection—it's a reckoning.

By the time Bruce recorded Nebraska in 1982, that reckoning had deepened. He was no longer just chronicling the struggles of his youth; he was turning inward, facing his own fears and contradictions. Nebraska was recorded alone, on a 4-track cassette recorder, in a small bedroom.

It was stripped of production, unfiltered, and haunting. The album was a far cry from the anthemic style that had made him a global icon with Born to Run and The River. But for Bruce, Nebraska wasn't a detour. It was a necessary return. A return to Freehold, to the boy he had been, and to the raw honesty that had always lived beneath the larger-than-life image.

Deliver Me from Nowhere

The 2025 film Deliver Me from Nowhere explores that very moment—when Bruce Springsteen, at the height of fame, turned away from the spotlight to make his quietest, most personal record.

The movie captures the solitude, tension, and emotional weight of those sessions in a way that echoes the spirit of Nebraska itself. Jeremy Allen White's portrayal of Bruce adds a depth that feels both cinematic and intimate, showing the cracks and vulnerability behind the myth. It's not a story of stardom. It's a story of isolation, introspection, and the choice to be vulnerable when the world expects volume.

Deliver Me from Nowhere reminds us that sometimes the loudest truths are whispered, and that even legends carry the scars of their past. To understand Nebraska, and to appreciate the film, you have to go back to Freehold. To the boy watching his father stare blankly at the kitchen table. To the young man walking its streets, filled with questions he couldn't yet put into words. That boy from Freehold never left. He just learned how to speak through song.

Hungry Heart, Restless Soul

Becoming The Boss

Before he became "The Boss," Bruce Springsteen was a hungry young artist from Freehold, New Jersey, with a guitar, a vision, and an unshakable belief that music could offer more than just entertainment. It could be salvation.

Raised in a working-class Catholic family, Springsteen grew up in a house where silence often said more than words, and where dreams seemed like something meant for someone else. But from an early age, Bruce felt something stir inside him. It was a restless energy that only music could calm. Inspired by Elvis Presley, The Beatles, and the grit of soul and R & B, Bruce began to write songs not to impress but to express.

His lyrics weren't just about love or rebellion. They were about escape, identity, and what it meant to come from somewhere that no one talked about unless they wanted to leave it. In the early 1970s, Springsteen signed with Columbia Records, and the label famously promoted him as the next Bob Dylan. That comparison, while flattering, was also limiting.

Dylan was cerebral. Bruce was visceral. He sang with the force of a man who knew what was at stake in every verse. His early albums, Greetings from Asbury Park, N.J. and The Wild, the Innocent & the E Street Shuffle, were critical darlings but commercial flops. Yet, they planted seeds. The poetry was there. So was the heart.

Then came Born to Run in 1975. The album changed everything. The title track exploded with energy and yearning. It wasn't just a song; it was a declaration. He wasn't just trying to get out of town—he was trying to carry the whole town with him. With Born to Run, Springsteen became The Boss, not by self-proclamation, but because audiences and critics alike sensed he had something to say, and he wasn't afraid to shout it from the stage.

But being The Boss came with expectations. There were record executives, media appearances, sold-out tours, and a growing pressure to keep delivering anthems for people who were just barely holding on. Bruce had become a voice for the blue-collar, the bruised, and the believers. It was a role he didn't take lightly. But as the spotlight grew hotter, so did the weight of carrying it.

Fame, Pressure, and the Cost of Success

With success came noise. The world wanted more of Bruce Springsteen—more albums, more interviews, more tours, more meaning. But fame isn't a natural condition. It warps reality and messes with your compass. For someone as intensely introspective as Springsteen, it started to take a toll.

The years following Born to Run were marked by both creative high points and personal struggles. Darkness on the Edge of Town showed that Bruce wasn't content to ride the wave of commercial success. He wanted to dig deeper. The songs were darker, stripped of the youthful optimism of his earlier work.

They spoke to disillusionment, frustration, and grit. But while the music matured, Bruce was wrestling with demons of his own—legal battles with his first manager, uncertainty about his place in the industry, and an internal conflict between staying authentic and living up to a carefully curated public image.

Fame started to feel like a trap. Interviews felt rehearsed. Tours became exhausting. Every record came with the burden of topping the last. Despite his image as a working-class hero, Bruce felt increasingly disconnected from the people he was supposed to represent. He had money, recognition, and influence—but he also felt empty.

That emptiness became fuel for something else entirely. In 1982, instead of heading back to the studio with the full E Street Band, Bruce stayed home. Armed with a 4-track cassette recorder and a guitar, he began to record what would become Nebraska in a small New Jersey bedroom. There was no producer, no flashy equipment, no studio magic. Just Springsteen, his voice, and the stories that had been weighing on him.

Nebraska was the opposite of a stadium anthem. The songs were bleak, often narrated by criminals, loners, and people lost to their own despair. It was a risk. Columbia Records was unsure how to market it. But for Bruce, it was more than an album. It was a purge. He needed to speak in a whisper because the roar of fame had become too loud.

Deliver Me from Nowhere captures this turning point. The film doesn't just document the making of Nebraska; it reveals what it cost Springsteen to make it. Jeremy Allen White's performance as Bruce is quiet, haunted, and powerful. He doesn't try to impersonate Springsteen. Instead, he inhabits the emotional space Bruce occupied during those years. Director Scott Cooper leans into the stillness. Long silences. Shadows. Scenes that feel more like memories than moments.

This wasn't the Springsteen of Born in the U.S.A.. This was a man searching for himself in the quiet corners of his mind. A restless soul tired of the noise. And in many ways, Nebraska became a mirror for the people who heard it. Stripped of production, fame, or fanfare, it asked a simple question: what do we become when no one is watching?

The pressure to succeed nearly crushed the man who once promised to pull everyone out of town in a car with a busted engine. But Bruce didn't just survive it. He transformed it into art. Deliver Me from Nowhere reminds us that sometimes, the most powerful work comes not when you're trying to be seen, but when you're finally ready to see yourself.

Ghosts on the Highway

Bruce and the Burden of Expectation

By the early 1980s, Bruce Springsteen was a household name. After the explosive success of Born to Run (1975) and the artistic credibility earned from Darkness on the Edge of Town (1978), Springsteen had firmly established himself as a figure who could both sell out stadiums and write songs that cut to the bone.

By 1980, The River showcased the duality of his identity: a man caught between rock anthems and aching ballads, between chart-topping success and deep artistic introspection. But success, for Bruce, didn't bring peace. In fact, it introduced an entirely new set of anxieties. He was no longer the scrappy underdog from New Jersey trying to break into the industry.

He was The Boss. And that title came with its own weight—a pressure to keep producing, to remain authentic, and to somehow stay connected to the very people whose lives he once mirrored in his lyrics. Springsteen felt the walls closing in. Fame had become a double-edged sword. On one hand, he had creative freedom, commercial success, and a loyal following. On the other, he feared losing the emotional core of his work.

He worried that the machine of fame might turn him into something manufactured. These weren't just personal fears; they were existential ones. What happens when a working-class poet becomes a millionaire? Can he still write about struggle without sounding false?

This burden was more than just philosophical. Bruce reportedly went through bouts of depression during this time, wrestling with self-doubt and restlessness. His performances remained electric, but offstage, the energy began to shift. He was searching for something—not another hit, but a sense of truth. And in a world that kept asking for more, louder, bigger—he began to crave less. Smaller. Simpler.

It's here, in this internal tug-of-war, that the seeds of Nebraska were sown. A desire to strip everything away and rediscover the raw core of his voice. And to do that, Bruce had to confront the ghosts he had accumulated along the highway of fame: the doubts, the expectations, and the quiet realization that success doesn't always feel like victory.

The Road That Led to Nebraska

Bruce Springsteen didn't set out to make an album like Nebraska. He didn't enter a state-of-the-art studio with a master plan. In fact, he didn't enter a studio at all. The songs that would become Nebraska were recorded on a 4-track cassette recorder in his bedroom in Colts Neck, New Jersey.

They weren't demos, though at first that's what he assumed they were. They were something different—more skeletal, more intimate, more haunted. The journey to those recordings began with disillusionment. In 1981, Springsteen was preparing for another E Street Band album. He had written a series of songs and was ready to begin rehearsals. But when he started putting those songs together with the band, something didn't sit right.

The heart of the songs—their emotional clarity—began to feel buried under layers of sound. They weren't bad; they just weren't honest in the way Bruce needed them to be. So he stepped back. Alone, with a guitar and harmonica, Bruce started recording the songs by himself. No band, no filters.

The result was startling. Songs like "Atlantic City," "Highway Patrolman," and "State Trooper" carried a weight that couldn't be replicated in a bigger production. They felt like short stories set to music—bleak, beautiful, and uncomfortably real.

Each track told the story of someone struggling at the edge of society: criminals, drifters, broken brothers, and weary fathers. It wasn't just the characters who were lost—Bruce was, too. These songs became his mirror. He was examining not just the world, but his place in it. The recording quality was rough, but that added to its honesty.

It felt like these songs weren't supposed to be heard by anyone else. They were private journal entries, pressed onto tape. When he eventually brought the recordings to his producer and tried re-recording them in a studio setting with the E Street Band, something was lost. The edge dulled. The tension eased. And Bruce knew he couldn't fake what he had captured alone in that room. The cassette demos became the album. Not by design, but by necessity.

Nebraska was released in 1982, and it stood in stark contrast to the high-gloss records dominating the charts at the time. There were no anthems here. No radio-friendly choruses. Just a man, his voice, and a collection of stories that refused to blink. It was bold in its quietness, radical in its restraint. And for Bruce Springsteen, it was a turning point.

It marked a moment when he stopped running. When he stopped trying to meet expectations and instead faced himself. The road that led to Nebraska wasn't paved with fame. It was lined with doubt, silence, and a restless search for truth. In the end, it led not to nowhere, but to something lasting. Something real.

And Deliver Me from Nowhere, both the book by Warren Zanes and the film inspired by it, tries to capture that truth—the story of a man stripping everything down so he could find his way back to what mattered most.

The Nebraska Sessions

Four Tracks and a Bedroom

By the early 1980s, Bruce Springsteen had reached the kind of success most artists only dream of. His 1980 double album, The River, had gone multi-platinum, and his live performances were selling out stadiums across the country. But behind the scenes, Springsteen was emotionally worn down.

The fame, the noise, the expectations—they weighed heavily on an artist whose creative core was rooted in quiet reflection and working-class storytelling. He felt disconnected, not just from the music industry, but from himself. This tension gave birth to what would become one of his most haunting and honest records: Nebraska.

It started in his home in Colts Neck, New Jersey. Springsteen wasn't chasing perfection or even intending to release what he was recording. He had a modest TEAC 144 four-track cassette recorder, a pair of Shure microphones, a harmonica, a twelve-string acoustic guitar, and a reel-to-reel tape deck.

The plan was simple: lay down rough demos for the full band to polish later. But what he captured in those first takes was more than sketches—they were raw, intimate, and fully formed. Springsteen recorded most of the songs in one session, sitting on his bed with the tape rolling.

There was no studio sheen, no backup vocals, no E Street Band. Just the man, his guitar, and the stories of drifters, killers, and loners drifting through a stark American landscape. Songs like "Atlantic City," "State Trooper," and "Highway Patrolman" were born in that space, filtered through Springsteen's fascination with noir literature, Terrence Malick films, and the haunting realism of Flannery O'Connor's writing.

What made these recordings extraordinary wasn't their sonic quality—it was the emotional resonance. You could hear the creak of the floorboards, the click of buttons, the faint hum of background noise. All of it contributed to the atmosphere. The intimacy was undeniable, and once Springsteen listened back to the cassette, he realized something vital: the demos weren't blueprints. They were the final product.

He brought the songs to the studio and attempted to recreate them with the E Street Band. But no matter how skilled the musicians were, something was lost in translation. The rawness was diluted. The ache and isolation that made the songs so powerful seemed to vanish under the polish of production. So Springsteen made a radical choice: he would release the cassette versions. The album was cleaned up just enough to be technically viable, but the core remained untouched.

Nebraska came out on September 30, 1982, and it stunned fans and critics alike. It was the sound of a man pulling back from the spotlight to confront his own shadows. The album didn't climb the charts like Born to Run or The River, but it carved out a place in the heart of American music as one of Springsteen's most fearless statements.

Why He Walked Away from the E Street Band (Temporarily)

The decision to record and release Nebraska solo wasn't just an artistic detour; it was a personal reckoning. At the time, Springsteen was struggling with his mental health. The sudden rush of success had left him feeling unmoored, and he questioned the version of himself that fame had created.

While the E Street Band was more than a backing group—they were his musical family—Springsteen knew he needed space to figure out who he was outside of the noise. He wasn't abandoning them; he was stepping back. His decision to work alone in Nebraska was a way to strip down not just the music, but his life. He needed the solitude to reconnect with the quieter truths that had always been his foundation.

The band understood, even if it wasn't easy. Max Weinberg later said in interviews that they all knew Bruce had to do what he had to do. There was a deep respect for his process. In many ways, Nebraska was a test of trust—in himself, in his audience, and in the belief that less could be more.

By stepping away from the band, Springsteen showed a different kind of bravery. Not the kind that comes from thunderous riffs and packed arenas, but the quiet courage it takes to be still and listen to your own doubts. The themes of Nebraska mirrored that internal struggle.

Many of the characters in the songs are isolated, morally conflicted, or on the edge of collapse. It was no coincidence. Springsteen channeled his own confusion and restlessness into those stories. The result was a body of work that felt both timeless and painfully current.

He would return to the E Street Band, of course. The break was temporary, but necessary. When he came back with Born in the U.S.A., it was with renewed purpose and clarity. The experience of creating Nebraska alone shaped not just his sound, but his soul.

And now, decades later, that quiet detour has become a landmark. The film Deliver Me from Nowhere doesn't just recount how an album was made. It dives into why it had to be made that way—in the stillness, in the solitude, and in the search for something real. Springsteen didn't walk away from the E Street Band because he lost faith in them.

He walked toward something he couldn't ignore: the voice in the silence.

⑤ Stories in the Static

The Characters of Nebraska: Killers, Drifters, and Dreamers

In 1982, Bruce Springsteen released an album that stripped away everything fans had come to expect from him. Nebraska wasn't an arena-rock declaration or a working-class anthem. It was a whisper.

A stark, haunted portrait of America's lost and disillusioned. And it told its stories not with a full band, but with a 4-track recorder in a New Jersey bedroom. The result? A collection of characters who don't just exist in songs—they haunt you.

What makes Nebraska so compelling is its refusal to look away. The characters in these songs are not caricatures. They're not elevated by metaphor or softened by sentiment. They're raw. Their motivations are often unclear. Their actions are sometimes unforgivable. And their situations? Hopeless, but human.

Take the title track, "Nebraska." Inspired by the real-life killing spree of Charles Starkweather and Caril Ann Fugate in the 1950s, the narrator speaks in a flat, emotionless tone about his crimes: "I can't say that I'm sorry for the things that we done." There's no redemption arc, no moralizing. Just a chilling kind of resignation. Springsteen isn't asking you to understand the killer. He's just asking you to sit with him for a while. And that's far more unsettling.

Then there's "Johnny 99," where a laid-off auto worker turns to crime and murder, then pleads for execution in court. What's disturbing isn't just what he does—it's how clearly he explains why he did it. It's an indictment of a system that leaves people with no choices and then punishes them for acting out of desperation.

In "Highway Patrolman," the story shifts to a small-town police officer and his brother. The officer lets his brother escape across the Canadian border after a violent act. It's not just about family loyalty—it's about a man torn between his duty and his love, and how impossible it is to live clean in a dirty world.

Not all the characters are violent, but they're all marked by some kind of loneliness. "Mansion on the Hill" is about a boy who can only dream of the life he watches from afar. "Used Cars" captures childhood shame and longing with devastating simplicity.

And "My Father's House" is a quiet meditation on memory, guilt, and the futile search for reconciliation. These aren't stories of triumph. They're stories of people slipping through the cracks. People you might never notice, but Springsteen did. And in Nebraska, he gave them a voice—quiet, but unflinching.

Stark Honesty as a Creative Choice

By the early 1980s, Springsteen had already become The Boss. Born to Run had made him a legend. The River had taken him to the top of the charts. He had the attention of the world. But with Nebraska, he chose silence over spectacle. He turned down the volume, turned off the spotlight, and turned inward.

The decision to record the album solo, on a 4-track recorder at home, was more than a technical choice. It was a statement. At a time when music was getting bigger, shinier, and more commercial, Springsteen made something small, bare, and intimate. He could have brought these songs into a studio, fleshed them out with the E Street Band. And he tried. But the spirit of the songs was lost in translation.

He kept the demos.

There's a certain bravery in that. Stripping away the polish means there's nowhere to hide. Every creak in his voice, every breath, every pause—it's all there. The flaws become the features. And in that rawness, you find something that feels truer than perfection.

Springsteen has often said that he writes to make sense of the world. With Nebraska, he wasn't trying to lead a charge or rally the troops. He was trying to understand the darkness. Where it comes from. What it does to people. And why it never fully goes away.

This stark honesty is what makes the album timeless. It doesn't rely on trends or production tricks. It doesn't offer easy answers. It just tells the truth, even when it's uncomfortable. And this is where Deliver Me from Nowhere—the upcoming film based on Warren Zanes' book—finds its emotional center. The movie isn't about hits or fame.

It's about the silence between the songs. The decision to lean into solitude. The fear that success might disconnect you from the very world you started writing about. Jeremy Allen White's portrayal of Springsteen focuses on these quiet moments. The writing. The long walks. The inner conversations.

The doubt. And ultimately, the artistic courage it takes to create something that might not please the crowd, but tells the truth you need to tell. That truth lives in every character on Nebraska. It lives in every breath on that tape. And now, it lives again—on film, for a new generation to hear the static and listen closer.

⑥

Reception and Reflection

Critics, Fans, and the Music Industry's Reaction

When Bruce Springsteen released Nebraska in 1982, the music world was bracing for another full-band blockbuster after the massive success of The River (1980). Instead, Springsteen delivered a sparse, lo-fi album recorded on a 4-track cassette recorder in his New Jersey bedroom.

It wasn't what anyone expected. The initial reactions were varied—some glowing, others confused—but everyone agreed: this wasn't just another Springsteen record.

Critical Response:

From the outset, Nebraska split critics. Rolling Stone praised its bravery, calling it "a chilling collection of American short stories" while The Village Voice described it as "a haunting departure from the myth-making

Springsteen." Many respected its raw minimalism and introspective content, though others questioned its commercial viability. Unlike his previous albums filled with anthemic energy, Nebraska was quiet, meditative, and often bleak. Yet, its stark storytelling and emotional honesty hit a nerve.

Robert Christgau gave it high marks for its "stunning artistic integrity," and Jon Pareles would later call it one of the most important albums of the decade. In the UK, the NME called it "a ghost record" and "the sound of America waking up from a dream it couldn't afford."

Fan Reaction:

For long-time fans, the album took some getting used to. Those drawn to Bruce's energetic live shows and E Street swagger were initially taken aback. But many eventually came to see Nebraska as one of his most intimate and meaningful works. It became a cult favorite—the kind of album people discover and cling to in their loneliest hours.

There were fan letters, stories, and even pilgrimages. Some listeners said it helped them through personal losses or mental health struggles. The themes of alienation, desperation, and fleeting hope spoke to anyone who'd ever felt isolated in a crowd.

Industry Response:

From a commercial standpoint, Nebraska was a gamble. Columbia Records was reportedly unsure about releasing such an unpolished album, especially when Bruce had recorded full-band versions of the same songs with the E Street Band. But Springsteen held his ground, believing in the power of the raw demos.

Though it didn't match the sales figures of The River or Born in the U.S.A., Nebraska performed respectably, going platinum and securing a Grammy nomination. It was also named Album of the Year by NME and ranked high in multiple year-end lists.

Ultimately, the music industry viewed Nebraska as a bold move. It wasn't business as usual, and that made it stand out. Other artists took notice. The album's influence soon began to ripple out through folk, indie, and even punk circles.

How Time Changed the Album's Legacy

In the years following its release, Nebraska transformed from an outlier to a benchmark. Initially seen as an artistic detour, it is now regarded as one of Springsteen's most important records—not in spite of its simplicity, but because of it.

Aging Gracefully:

What once puzzled audiences now feels prophetic. Nebraska anticipated the rise of lo-fi, bedroom recordings that became staples in indie music decades later. In a world obsessed with polish and perfection, Nebraska endures as a reminder that authenticity always outlives production value.

Its raw honesty has aged well, especially in a cultural landscape that increasingly values transparency and vulnerability. In many ways, it was ahead of its time.

Influence on Artists and Genres:

You can hear echoes of Nebraska in the work of artists like Bon Iver, Sufjan Stevens, The National, and even Johnny Cash's later American recordings with Rick Rubin. The album's influence transcended genre.

Alt-country, gothic Americana, and lo-fi folk artists frequently cite it as foundational. Ben Gibbard of Death Cab for Cutie once said, "Without Nebraska, I don't know that a lot of us would even have the vocabulary to write the kind of songs we do."

Reevaluated by Critics:

Many critics who were lukewarm at first came to see Nebraska in a new light. Its stature grew with each passing year. In Rolling Stone's updated "500 Greatest Albums of All Time," it climbed steadily, eventually cracking the top 150. Mojo and Uncut both dedicated anniversary issues to its legacy.

Embraced by New Generations:

As digital platforms introduced Nebraska to new listeners, younger fans found themselves drawn to its timeless themes: alienation, disillusionment, the search for meaning. In an era of curated identities and highlight reels, the stark honesty of Nebraska resonates more than ever.

Playlists, YouTube comments, and Reddit threads overflow with testimonials: "This album feels like someone finally put my sadness into words." "I listened to this at 2 AM and felt like I understood."

The Movie Tie-In:

With the upcoming release of Deliver Me from Nowhere, interest in Nebraska is expected to surge again. The film not only introduces the album to wider audiences but gives context to its creation—deepening the appreciation for what Springsteen achieved in that small bedroom studio.

Early screenings suggest the movie does justice to the emotional weight of the record. Jeremy Allen White's portrayal and Scott Cooper's direction bring a new dimension to the man behind the music.

Nebraska may have arrived quietly, but it refused to be forgotten. Its reception was mixed at first, but with time it earned its place as a defining work not just for Springsteen, but for American music. What began as a personal exorcism in a quiet room has become a cultural landmark. And now, through film, it enters yet another chapter. Sometimes the loudest statements are whispered. Nebraska proved that. And the world finally listened.

Deliver Me from Nowhere — Book to Screen

Warren Zanes and the Source Material

Every story has an origin, and for Deliver Me from Nowhere, the seed was planted by author and music historian Warren Zanes. Known for his deep, accessible writing on music and its intersection with culture, Zanes approached Bruce Springsteen's Nebraska with both admiration and restraint.

What resulted was not a conventional biography, but something closer to a psychological excavation. Zanes' book Deliver Me from Nowhere: The Making of Bruce Springsteen's Nebraska was released in 2023 and quickly earned praise for its nuanced, intimate look at an album that had long eluded mainstream understanding.

Where most rock writing leans into chart success or tour highlights, Zanes turned inward—toward Springsteen's personal reckoning during a time of creative risk and emotional volatility. He treated Nebraska not as a product but as a moment of radical self-expression, a raw collection of demos that, against all expectations, became one of Springsteen's most revered works. What makes Zanes' book compelling is how he blends biography, journalism, and reflection.

Through interviews with Springsteen himself, members of the E Street Band, producers, and longtime confidants, Zanes gives readers a window into the mind of an artist standing at a crossroads. In these pages, we see a man struggling with fame, haunted by childhood trauma, and seeking a creative outlet that couldn't be reached through stadium-sized anthems.

The book doesn't treat Nebraska as a side project or a detour. Instead, it presents the album as central to understanding Springsteen's career and identity. That framing was crucial when it came time to translate the book to the screen.

Without Zanes' careful narrative balance—one that refused to sensationalize or oversimplify—the film adaptation might have felt hollow or performative. Instead, it had a foundation steeped in empathy, history, and human complexity.

Adapting a Quiet Story for the Big Screen

Turning a book like Zanes' Deliver Me from Nowhere into a film is no easy task. Unlike explosive biographies filled with drug binges and tabloid scandals, Nebraska is a story about internal struggle, creative solitude, and silence—all of which can be difficult to represent visually.

The job of capturing that quiet without making it boring fell to writer-director Scott Cooper, known for films like Crazy Heart and Hostiles. Cooper brought with him a talent for portraying characters in emotional isolation, which turned out to be a perfect match.

Jeremy Allen White's casting as Bruce Springsteen was an inspired choice. Best known for his intense, understated work on The Bear, White embodied Bruce not as a legend, but as a man wrestling with ghosts.

His performance wasn't built on mimicry; it was rooted in vulnerability. He doesn't play Springsteen as a rock god. He plays him as a guy in a bedroom with a guitar, unsure if the music he's making will ever see daylight. That restraint anchors the film. Visually, the film reflects the lo-fi aesthetic of Nebraska. Shot in subdued tones and often framed in wide, quiet compositions, it resists modern biopic conventions.

There are no stadium concerts, no rags-to-riches montages. Instead, we get cold highways, blank notebooks, brief phone calls, and moments of silence that stretch just long enough to feel real. The camera lingers where most would cut. Dialogue is sparse but meaningful. Music is used with care, appearing like punctuation rather than wallpaper.

Adaptation also meant deciding what not to show. Deliver Me from Nowhere doesn't chronicle Bruce's entire life or even his broader discography. It hones in on the creative moment around Nebraska. That narrow focus, borrowed from Zanes' book, gives the film depth instead of breadth.

It allows the audience to dwell in the same discomfort and introspection that Springsteen faced during that winter in New Jersey. Scott Cooper reportedly consulted Zanes throughout the adaptation, and their shared respect for Bruce's boundaries shaped the film's tone.

Springsteen himself had limited involvement, visiting the set and offering guidance without dominating the process. His presence lingered, but his silence spoke volumes. The result is a film that honors its subject without turning him into a myth.

What the movie achieves—and what many adaptations fail to do—is match the emotional tempo of its source. It does not rush. It does not glorify. It listens.

In many ways, adapting Deliver Me from Nowhere was about trusting the quiet. It was about letting stillness hold the weight of a man's creative truth. Just as the album Nebraska found power in restraint, so too does the film that bears its name. And just as Warren Zanes wrote with insight instead of intrusion, the filmmakers followed suit, crafting something that feels less like a performance and more like a memory.

Casting the Legend

Jeremy Allen White as Bruce Springsteen

Casting someone to play Bruce Springsteen isn't just about finding a good actor. It's about finding a presence, a weight, a silence, and a fire. That balance is rare, and that's what makes Jeremy Allen White's casting in Deliver Me from Nowhere so fascinating—and risky.

Known primarily for his role as Carmy in The Bear, White stepped into Springsteen's skin during one of the most vulnerable chapters of the musician's life. And he did it not with bombast or mimicry, but with restraint, grounding, and a deep respect for the real man behind the myth.

The decision to cast White was met with curiosity and some skepticism. How could a contemporary TV star convincingly portray the Boss? But the moment the trailer dropped, it was clear that something unexpected was happening. Jeremy Allen White didn't try to impersonate Springsteen—he interpreted him.

His physical transformation was impressive, but more crucially, he captured the emotional core: a man isolated by success, disoriented by fame, and reaching inward for something honest. The kind of internal weight that Nebraska carried in every line and every note. White trained intensively for the role, not just vocally but physically.

His guitar playing, posture, speech rhythm, and even his silences were carefully studied. But what made his performance magnetic was the lived-in pain and detachment he brought to screen. In interviews, White admitted to having his own complicated relationship with pressure, identity, and performance, and that truth bled into his portrayal of Bruce.

One particularly haunting moment in the film shows Springsteen recording into a 4-track in a darkened room, unsure if what he's doing is madness or genius. White holds that tension masterfully. He doesn't overplay it. He doesn't beg for empathy. He just is. That kind of performance is rare in music biopics, which often lean toward hagiography or theatricality.

White instead honors Springsteen by showing him as a man in quiet crisis, struggling to reconcile the roaring stadium icon with the solitary songwriter haunted by his own past. Director Scott Cooper said that White brought an "unnerving focus" to the role—a quiet intensity that fit the tone of the film and the emotional spirit of the album it explores.

Springsteen himself reportedly visited the set a few times and was said to be impressed, noting White as a "terrific actor" who "gets it." What makes this performance even more daring is that White sings in the film. Not in an attempt to replicate the stadium thunder of "Born in the U.S.A.," but the raw acoustic intimacy of Nebraska.

In early test screenings, viewers noted how the fragility in his voice made certain scenes feel even more personal, even more dangerous in their stillness. It wasn't perfect—and that was the point. Neither was Nebraska. It was authentic.

In a year full of loud movies and louder performances, Jeremy Allen White's Bruce Springsteen is a whisper that echoes. And it may just be his most defining performance to date.

Portraying Real People with Weight and Accuracy

Biographical films are a minefield. They have to honor the subject without idolizing them, represent the truth without turning it into documentary, and dramatize events without cheapening them. For Deliver Me from Nowhere, the stakes were even higher.

Bruce Springsteen isn't just a famous musician; he's an American archetype. He's mythologized in lyrics, politics, and cultural memory. So portraying him with real emotional weight and accuracy required not just good casting but a disciplined creative vision.

The film doesn't aim to show Springsteen as the rock god. It doesn't rehash the big concerts or the rise to fame. It zooms in on a narrow, haunting window of his life—the recording of Nebraska in 1982.

This was a moment where he consciously stepped away from commercial success and instead chased something raw and interior. That choice defines the tone of the entire film. It's not about the hits. It's about the silences in between them. What gives the film weight is its refusal to explain too much.

It lets Bruce's world be what it was: dim, quiet, uneasy. Jeremy Strong's performance as manager Jon Landau is equally restrained, serving as both a sounding board and a counterpoint. The dynamic between them is subtle but essential—Springsteen was not navigating this creative crisis alone, but it felt like he was.

Accuracy came through in the details. The film closely follows the known timeline of how the Nebraska album was created: the cassette recordings, the decision not to re-record with the E Street Band, and the internal struggle Springsteen faced over whether to release such a stark, personal project.

It avoids overdramatizing or adding fictional conflicts. Instead, it lets the truth do the heavy lifting. The art direction and cinematography support that weight. Settings are bare, lighting is minimal, and everything has a textured, analog feel. It's not just a nod to the early '80s but a way to visually reflect the stripped-down aesthetic of the album.

The storytelling moves slowly, even uncomfortably at times, mirroring how Nebraska forces its listeners to sit with unease. Portraying a real person means embracing the contradictions. Bruce was famous, but lonely. Celebrated, but unsure. Gifted, but deeply troubled by ghosts he couldn't shake. The film doesn't resolve these tensions, nor should it.

It presents Springsteen as he was during that moment: a man not quite at peace with himself, turning to music not to escape, but to make sense of what he couldn't outrun. In that way, Deliver Me from Nowhere succeeds where many biopics fail. It doesn't give you a hero. It gives you a human. And through Jeremy Allen White's performance and the film's careful attention to emotional truth, it delivers a story that lingers long after the credits roll.

Inside the Film

Scene by Scene: What the Film Shows

Deliver Me from Nowhere doesn't unfold like a typical music biopic. Instead of focusing on the sweep of Bruce Springsteen's entire life or the greatest hits of his career, the film narrows in on one intense, transformative moment: the making of Nebraska.

This decision immediately sets it apart, and scene by scene, it draws us into a quieter, more introspective narrative. The film opens with a subdued montage of early morning shots in New Jersey. Fog over empty fields, trucks passing by in the distance, Bruce walking alone with a guitar case in hand.

There is no voiceover, no dramatic exposition—only silence and subtle movement. The atmosphere is thick with isolation, visually echoing the emotional landscape that Nebraska would later express. This opening sets the tone: we are entering not a glamorous rise-to-fame story, but the internal retreat of a man confronting his limits.

Jeremy Allen White's portrayal of Springsteen begins here, wordlessly. He doesn't rush into performance; he lingers in solitude. The first scenes show Bruce avoiding the studio, driving aimlessly, sitting in diners without speaking. We get a glimpse into his restlessness, his inability to channel his energy into anything public or performative. This slow burn introduces the emotional block he's experiencing. Fame hasn't solved anything—it has only made the ghosts louder.

From there, the film gradually begins to fill in the picture. Scenes at his parents' house show strained but tender interactions with his father, played by Stephen Graham. There are moments of unresolved tension, but also flickers of understanding. The screenplay wisely avoids over-explaining their relationship, trusting gestures, silences, and looks to do the heavy lifting.

The heart of the film revolves around Bruce's makeshift home recording setup. In these dimly lit scenes, we see Springsteen recording track after track, alone. Jeremy Allen White delivers understated power here. There's no montage of artistic triumphs. Instead, we watch the repetition, the trial and error, the quiet self-doubt.

The camera lingers on his face as he listens to the playback of "My Father's House" and "State Trooper," uncertain if he's capturing truth or just noise. Intercut with these recording sessions are brief, haunting sequences of the characters that populate the Nebraska songs. A man stares into a rearview mirror, bloodied. A woman walks barefoot along a desolate road.

These are dreamlike vignettes, not literal interpretations, giving visual texture to the themes Springsteen explores: moral ambiguity, loneliness, guilt, and grace. We also get glimpses of Bruce's collaborators reacting to the early tapes. His manager, Jon Landau (played by Jeremy Strong), appears in a particularly strong scene where he listens, alone, to a rough cassette.

He is stunned, maybe even confused. "This isn't what people want," he says. "But it might be what they need." As the film progresses, the emotional weight builds. We learn through implication and subtle cues about Bruce's battle with depression, his struggle with perfectionism, and his fear that even his rawest work might miss the mark.

There is a standout moment when he sits in his car after recording, listening to "Reason to Believe" on cassette. He doesn't speak. He just cries. The final act doesn't offer a big triumphant conclusion. Instead, it gives us quiet resolution. Bruce mails the demo to Landau. He walks through a crowd unrecognized. The last shot is of him back in his room, not celebrating but simply sitting in the silence he's now made peace with.

What It Leaves Out — and Why

What's striking about Deliver Me from Nowhere is not just what it includes, but what it chooses to leave out. This is not the story of Bruce Springsteen the superstar, the E Street Band, or even the larger cultural moment of the early 1980s.

The film leaves out the stadiums, the screaming fans, and even the broader press narrative around the album Nebraska. And it does so deliberately. One of the most notable omissions is the absence of live performance footage. We never see Bruce on stage. This choice reinforces the film's central premise: Nebraska wasn't born under spotlights.

It came out of darkness, solitude, and doubt. To show concerts would dilute that focus. The E Street Band is mentioned but not featured. Max Weinberg, Little Steven, Clarence Clemons—none of them appear as characters. In a typical Springsteen biopic, this would be a glaring hole. Here, it's purposeful. Nebraska was the rare moment Bruce stepped away from the band, both literally and emotionally. The film honors that separation.

Also left out is a detailed timeline of Bruce's prior successes. There's no flashback to "Born to Run" or "The River." The film assumes its viewer already understands who Bruce is. This allows the story to breathe within the limited frame of the Nebraska sessions, rather than getting caught in fan-service or Greatest Hits territory.

There's also little direct reference to political or cultural commentary—a hallmark of Springsteen's public persona. But this is not a film about Bruce the activist. It's about Bruce the man, and how that man wrestled with his own voice when it suddenly sounded unfamiliar.

Why does the film make these omissions? Because its strength lies in restraint. It aims to capture one thing, and do it fully. The result is a focused character study, a rare portrait of an artist not at his peak but on the edge of something uncertain and unfiltered.

In doing so, Deliver Me from Nowhere becomes something few biopics achieve: an emotionally authentic echo of the work it was inspired by. Like Nebraska, it whispers rather than shouts. And in that silence, it finds something real.

Direction and Style

Scott Cooper's Vision

When a director takes on the challenge of capturing a figure like Bruce Springsteen, there's no room for shortcuts. Scott Cooper, known for his contemplative and character-driven storytelling (Crazy Heart, Out of the Furnace, Hostiles), approached Deliver Me from Nowhere not as a traditional music biopic, but as a human story with a quiet, aching pulse.

He wasn't interested in chart-topping hits or backstage glamour. He was interested in solitude, silence, and the creative battle that unfolds when an artist is left alone with his thoughts. That focus would define every frame of this film.

Cooper's direction leans heavily into the atmosphere of Nebraska itself: sparse, haunting, and deeply personal. He reportedly told his team from the beginning, "This isn't a story about a rock star. It's about a man trying to understand himself."

Instead of delivering a chronological, event-driven narrative, Cooper's storytelling is nonlinear and meditative. Flashbacks are used not for exposition, but as emotional echoes. Moments from Bruce's childhood, fractured memories of his father, and internal dialogues surface like static on a tape. The camera doesn't rush; it lingers.

We see Bruce, played with quiet intensity by Jeremy Allen White, often sitting in silence, staring out a window or walking through the Jersey winter. These still moments invite the viewer into the kind of personal space rarely captured in biographical cinema. Cooper also resists the temptation of hagiography.

His Bruce Springsteen is not a mythic figure—he's a man struggling with ghosts, doubts, and pressure. The film leans into Bruce's emotional exhaustion after The River tour and explores his quiet rejection of the rock persona he had created. Rather than romanticizing Springsteen's decision to record Nebraska alone on a 4-track in his bedroom, Cooper presents it as a creative necessity—a desperate act of expression.

Crucially, Cooper involved Springsteen throughout the filmmaking process but maintained enough distance to preserve the artistic integrity of the project. Bruce reportedly gave advice, shared personal insights, and even visited the set, but chose not to interfere in direction. This balance allowed Cooper to capture a version of Springsteen that felt emotionally authentic while giving the actor space to interpret the role freely.

Mood, Color, and Cinematic Silence

The mood of Deliver Me from Nowhere is arguably its most defining trait. Much like the Nebraska album itself, the film is stark, minimal, and meditative. It speaks in quiet tones. There are no grand crescendos, no sweeping orchestral backdrops, and no Hollywood gloss.

What you get instead is silence, broken only by acoustic strums, the occasional hum of a radiator, or the distant sound of wind against a windowpane. Cinematographer Masanobu Takayanagi, who has worked with Cooper before, crafts a visual language built on muted tones and natural light.

Interiors are bathed in soft grays and browns, giving a sense of both warmth and emotional weight. Exteriors are often overcast, filmed in the colder months to replicate the rawness of Bruce's New Jersey surroundings in the early '80s. The film avoids the golden hues often used in period pieces and opts instead for a restrained, wintery palette that feels closer to documentary than drama.

There is a deliberateness to every visual choice. The 4:3 aspect ratio used in some sequences mirrors old home footage, subtly evoking nostalgia and isolation. Grain is added to certain scenes to reflect the lo-fi texture of the Nebraska recordings. At times, the visuals feel more like still photography than motion picture—framed and frozen to force reflection.

Lighting is low and intimate. Shadows are used not just for aesthetic contrast but to reflect the inner fragmentation of the character. In scenes where Bruce is composing alone, light sources often come from a single lamp or the gray light of dawn. These choices strip away the polish, leaving the viewer with a sense of raw immediacy.

Sound design also plays a crucial role. In a world obsessed with noise, Deliver Me from Nowhere does the unthinkable: it embraces quiet. Dialogue is sparse, and there are long sequences where not a word is spoken. When music does appear, it feels earned, and never overbearing. Jeremy Allen White, who performs the songs himself, delivers them with a cracked intimacy that complements the visuals rather than overpowering them.

The pacing, too, is unhurried. Scenes are allowed to breathe. There's a confidence in the silence—an understanding that sometimes, the lack of sound can say more than any monologue. This quiet is where the film lives. It creates space for the audience to not just observe, but feel.

Together, Scott Cooper's direction and the film's cinematic mood form a cohesive, emotionally intelligent portrait of an artist on the edge. Deliver Me from Nowhere doesn't shout; it whispers. And in that whisper, it manages to say everything it needs to about art, doubt, and the power of stillness.

The Sound of Nebraska Reimagined

Music Direction and Live Performances in the Film

Reimagining the sound of Bruce Springsteen's Nebraska for a modern film adaptation was never going to be simple. The original album, recorded on a humble 4-track cassette recorder in Springsteen's bedroom, is steeped in minimalism and emotional weight.

Translating that into a cinematic setting required a thoughtful approach that would respect the stark, haunting tone of the album while adapting it to the demands of a visual medium. It was not just a matter of inserting music into scenes—it was about building an auditory atmosphere that captured the core of Springsteen's artistic moment in 1982.

Director Scott Cooper, known for his work on films like Crazy Heart and Hostiles, collaborated closely with music supervisors and sound designers to ensure that the emotional DNA of Nebraska was preserved. Rather than embellish or orchestrate the songs, the team leaned into the rawness. In fact, one of the earliest creative decisions was to maintain the lo-fi aesthetic.

Ambient noise, tape hiss, and the bare-bones acoustic quality were carefully replicated to feel authentic rather than polished. Jeremy Allen White, cast as Springsteen, took on the bold task of performing several songs live on set. It was a risk, but one that paid off. Rather than pre-recording studio-polished vocals and syncing to them during filming, White's live performances added an immediacy that echoes the urgency and intimacy of the original Nebraska sessions.

Viewers aren't just watching an actor play Springsteen—they're hearing a man alone in a room, with nothing but a guitar, a microphone, and his thoughts. That's the essence of Nebraska, and the film captures it with surprising fidelity. A standout moment comes in the film's rendition of "State Trooper."

The song, driven by Springsteen's whispered vocals and tense guitar strumming, is presented in near-total darkness, both visually and sonically. White performs the track almost in a whisper, mirroring the mood of dread and desperation that runs through the original recording. Instead of building a lush cinematic score around the scene, the filmmakers stripped everything away.

You hear the scrape of fingers on strings, the creak of floorboards. It's quiet, even uncomfortably so. But it works—because Nebraska is uncomfortable. Another key track, "Highway Patrolman," was reimagined not with grand visuals but through restraint. The emotional gravity of the song is allowed to unfold in a single extended take, with White delivering the lyrics in-character, seated alone at a kitchen table.

It's a moment that feels lived-in, almost like found footage. The direction trusts the song to carry the scene, and White's subdued delivery reflects the inner conflict of a man watching his brother spiral out of control. This commitment to authenticity extended into the sound mixing and mastering.

The audio team employed analog filters and vintage mics to get closer to the original timbre of Springsteen's voice and guitar tone. They even introduced slight imperfections—minor tuning inconsistencies, breath pops, and natural reverb from real rooms rather than digital simulations. The goal wasn't perfection—it was truth. Nebraska is about fractured people living in imperfect worlds, and the music had to reflect that.

Reinterpreting the Album for a New Audience

For many viewers, particularly younger generations, Deliver Me from Nowhere will be their first encounter with the Nebraska album. That presents a challenge and an opportunity: How do you make a 40-year-old lo-fi folk-rock album resonate with audiences raised on high-definition production and algorithm-curated playlists? The answer lies not in changing Nebraska, but in contextualizing it.

The film doesn't attempt to modernize the music in the traditional sense. There are no remixes, no pop features, no swelling orchestras. Instead, it brings new relevance to the themes that Nebraska so powerfully captured: isolation, moral conflict, working-class struggle, and the haunting silence of the American heartland. These are not outdated concepts—they are timeless, and arguably more pressing today than ever. The reinterpretation begins with character focus. By showing Bruce Springsteen's mental and emotional state during the making of the album—his depression, his disenchantment with fame, and his need to retreat into something raw—the film provides viewers with a lens through which to hear the songs differently.

This emotional framing makes it easier for new listeners to engage with Nebraska not just as music, but as testimony. To bridge generational gaps, the film also includes subtle narrative cues and visual storytelling that mirror the album's themes. For example, scenes set in wide, desolate landscapes echo the empty highways described in "Used Cars" and "Reason to Believe."

The characters in the film are often shown alone, facing away from the camera, lost in thought—just like the narrators of Nebraska's songs. These techniques don't alter the music, but they enhance its accessibility.

Some of the most powerful reinterpretations come through Jeremy Allen White's performance. He doesn't try to "do" Bruce. He doesn't impersonate the voice or the mannerisms. Instead, he delivers the songs with emotional sincerity, which strips away the layer of legend that sometimes obscures Springsteen's more intimate work.

In doing so, White reintroduces Nebraska to a new audience as not just a Bruce Springsteen album, but as a human story told through music. The release of the film has also inspired new interest in Springsteen's acoustic material. Streaming numbers for Nebraska saw a measurable uptick following the trailer's debut, and younger fans began discovering the album's quiet power.

Social media platforms, particularly TikTok and Instagram, have seen short clips from the film paired with Springsteen lyrics, often by users who had never posted about his music before. In a way, the film has become an unexpected cultural bridge, connecting past and present through the shared language of emotional truth.

In the end, Deliver Me from Nowhere doesn't reinvent Nebraska—it reintroduces it. By honoring the original sound while crafting a new emotional context, the film allows Bruce Springsteen's most stripped-down work to reach new ears and new hearts. It proves that sometimes, the quietest albums speak the loudest, especially when the world finally slows down long enough to listen.

Real vs. Represented
Where the Film Stays True

1. *Focusing on the Nebraska Sessions*

The film's central strength lies in its unwavering spotlight on Springsteen's 1982 Nebraska sessions—recorded alone in his Colts Neck, New Jersey, bedroom using a simple TEAC four-track cassette recorder.

That decision to capture the creation in a modest, claustrophobic setting aligns precisely with reality: the raw intimacy, crackling hiss, and even the slight equipment warbles are not cinematic embellishments—they are historically accurate, essential to the soul of the songs.

Visually and emotionally, the film recreates the tension of an artist caught between the razor's edge of raw inspiration and polished superstardom. Scott Cooper, drawing from Warren Zanes's book, duplicates scenes like Springsteen burning through 15 tracks in one night—10 making it to the album and others evolving into Born in the U.S.A. songs

2. Accurate Portrayals of Key People

A major achievement is the film's faithful depiction of the people who shaped that moment: Jon Landau, Springsteen's manager who supported—and later tried to refine—the Nebraska tapes, is portrayed with nuance by Jeremy Strong.

Mike Batlan, the guitar tech who operated the TEAC machine and witnessed the sessions firsthand, is included as an essential character, per Zanes's interviews.

Producers like Chuck Plotkin and execs like Al Teller make believable on-screen appearances, each tied to details in Zanes's book and contemporary reporting.

3. Springsteen's Emotional State

The movie's portrayal of Bruce grappling with loneliness, creative anxiety, and the weight of fame is grounded in the candid reflections found in Zanes's interviews and elsewhere. Particularly telling is the depiction of his relationship with his father, Douglas—marked by both love and unease—brought to life through Stephen Graham's nuanced performance, which matches Bruce's own lifelong struggle with generational trauma.

Bruce himself praised Jeremy Allen White's portrayal, especially in intimate scenes, and chose to absent himself from some emotionally intense shoots to maintain authenticity.

4. *Asbury Park & Jersey Backdrop*
Filming on location in Asbury Park, the Stone Pony, and other familiar Jersey landmarks adds another layer of realism. Films centered on this era often rely on stand-ins, but here, the production went the extra mile—period cars, storefronts, even carnival rides—to recreate Springsteen's early 1980s world in vivid detail.

5. *Music Quality and Performance*
The soundtrack doesn't just mimic; it embraces the flaws. Jeremy Allen White didn't lip-sync—he sang live, recreating the raw sound quality of the original demos. When Bruce visited the set, he praised White's performance as "wonderfully tolerant," affirming the authenticity of both voice and emotion.

Creative Liberties and What They Mean

Even the most faithful adaptations must shape reality for narrative flow, pacing, and dramatic tension. Deliver Me from Nowhere takes several creative liberties—and understanding their intent helps readers and viewers appreciate both the film and the real story more fully.

1. Compression of Timeline

The Nebraska sessions spanned several days in early January 1982. For clarity, the film condenses this process into a single, tension-filled night—an effective storytelling tactic, though not strictly chronological.

Real-world studio attempts and the decision to abandon full-band versions took longer and involved multiple discussions between Bruce and Landau. The film rounds these days into emblematic scenes to keep momentum and emotional weight at the forefront.

2. Heightened Emotional Confrontations

Screenwriters often simplify complex emotions into concise, powerful exchanges. In the film, Bruce may engage in a single, charged conversation with Landau or his father—whereas in reality, these were drawn-out, nuanced relational threads over weeks or months . This dramatic focus sacrifices some subtlety, but it also gives audiences emotional anchor points that highlight what Nebraska represented for Bruce.

3. Merged or Invented Composite Characters
Some characters may be composites or drawn from multiple real-life influences. For instance, minor producers or studio staff might be combined into a single "studio engineer" figure, adding clarity at the risk of factual purity. While there's no indication of egregious character fictions in public coverage, weariness with legal disclaimers suggests these blends enhance drama without bending trust.

4. Dramatic Visual Style
Director Scott Cooper employs stark color grading, strategic silence, and deliberate camera spacing to evoke the bleakness of the recordings. While emotionally accurate, these choices are cinematic rather than documentary. It's a creative amplification of mood, not a distortion—something Bruce reportedly recognized when he said in interviews the film "captures the emotional truth" even if scenes were simplified.

5. Narration vs. Dialogue

The book uses Bruce's own words as remembered or paraphrased by Zanes, which can't be used verbatim in the film. As a result, some dialogue is imagined. For example, Bruce's internal rationale during key decisions ("I won't take the band in; this is too personal") might be voiced aloud to guide viewers. These are creative interpolations—not falsehoods, but reminders that this is a biopic, not a verbatim documentary.

6. Omission of Certain Songs or Events

The film appears to sideline tracks that later evolved into Born in the U.S.A., such as "Born in the U.S.A." itself. While major songs like "Atlantic City" and "State Trooper" feature prominently, some fans will notice the absence of transitional numbers that illustrate the link between Nebraska and Bruce's next commercial triumph. This editorial decision centers the story on Nebraska as a self-contained artistic moment—but it leaves out the broader context of Bruce's career trajectory.

What the Creative Liberties Mean for Viewers and Fans

1. Emotional Truth Over Literal Truth

By keeping the Nebraska session focused and intense—sometimes at the expense of historical accuracy—the film heightens emotional resonance. Viewers experience the ache, tension, and urgency as if they're inside Bruce's mind that night.

2. Clarity for Wider Audiences

A biopic must engage new fans, moviegoers who aren't Springsteen disciples. Simplifying timelines and deepening the emotional arcs creates a more direct narrative. For many viewers, their takeaway will be: Nebraska was a moment of raw confrontation with self—and that's true.

3. An Invitation to Explore Beyond

Because the film doesn't cram in every story beat, curious fans are encouraged to read Warren Zanes's book, revisit studio recordings, or explore Bruce's interviews. In that sense, adaptation equals invitation—a springboard into deeper discovery.

4. Bridging Art and Commerce

One of the central tensions: Bruce faced a career-defining choice between artistic risk (Nebraska) and commercial potential (Born in the U.S.A.). The film chooses to dramatize that tension even more sharply, sometimes at the expense of nuance (e.g., leaving out Jon Landau's full faith). Viewers sense the stakes clearly—and that sparks conversation and appreciation for Bruce's risk-taking.

5. On Authenticity and Fictional Enhancement

Bruce Springsteen's own reception makes this notable. He praised White's performance as hitting emotional vérité, accepted directorial flourishes in tense scenes, and even allowed himself to stay off-screen to protect the authenticity of moments.

Balancing Act of Fact and Feeling

In the "Real vs. Represented" frame, Deliver Me from Nowhere" accomplishes something few biopics do: it respects the emotional core of a significant artistic moment while crafting a narratively tight film. It doesn't pretend to be a journalistic recounting of daily logs—it's focused.

It doesn't weigh you down with every who's who from the studio; instead, it drops you deep into a couple of key relationships. It doesn't include Bruce's full discography; it includes only the songs that matter in that room.

The creative liberties—compressed timelines, composite characters, polished visuals—serve one primary purpose: to maintain the film's emotional clarity and thematic resonance. The film says: Nebraska night. Creative fracture. Artistic breakthrough. Personal reckoning. That's the experience; the real-world details are still there, but they serve the psychology.

Suggested Next Steps for Readers

If You Want	Try This
To verify "what happened when"	*Read Warren Zanes's Deliver Me From Nowhere, which lays out day-by-day details and multiple interviews with Bruce, Landau, Batlan, and others*

To hear the original demos	*Track down cassette-source or early CD pressing of Nebraska. Listen for the hiss, the room, the mistakes—not the polished re-recordings*
To explore linkages with Born in the U.S.A.	*Compare the themes and characters across both albums—they form a creative diptych during one transformative period*
To spot cinematic choices	*Rewatch the film—when it goes silent, when scenes shift between bed-room and studio, when wide cuts isolate Bruce—note how tone guides understanding more than exposition*

Deliver Me from Nowhere may surrender certain details—exact dates, full band politics, even some peripheral figures—but it honors the emotional truth of the Nebraska chapter. In doing so, it becomes more than adaptation; it becomes a living, breathing portrait of an artist at a creative crossroads.

The film doesn't just show Bruce Springsteen recording an album—it invites the viewer into his loneliness, his courage, and the raw breakthrough that led not just to an album, but to an artistic turning point.

If the goal of any biography or guide is to inform—and if the goal of a movie is to move—Deliver Me from Nowhere succeeds at both. And acknowledging what's real, what's dramatized, and why, gives fans and newcomers a richer appreciation for Nebraska—and the man who made it.

Legacy and the Long View

Why Nebraska Still Matters

When Bruce Springsteen released Nebraska in 1982, it arrived as a whisper in the era of anthems. Coming off the commercial success of The River, expectations leaned toward another radio-friendly rock album filled with power chords and stadium-ready hooks.

What fans received instead was a stark, acoustic meditation on isolation, guilt, violence, and redemption. It was recorded solo, on a humble 4-track cassette recorder, in a bedroom in Colts Neck, New Jersey. The result was a haunting collection of songs that resisted the polish of commercial production, offering instead something raw, honest, and deeply human.

Over four decades later, Nebraska remains as relevant as ever. In fact, it matters more now in a world where music is often overproduced and emotionally detached. Nebraska reminds us what storytelling sounds like when stripped to its bare essentials. There are no distractions—just a voice, a guitar, and a man grappling with the country he loves and the characters who live in its shadows.

Thematically, Nebraska stands as a document of the American psyche at a time of transition. The album speaks to the disillusionment of the working class, the moral complexity of everyday choices, and the loneliness that often accompanies modern life. These themes continue to echo in contemporary culture, making Nebraska not only a product of its time but also a mirror held up to ours.

Musically, it also carved a path for lo-fi and alt-country artists who found in its imperfections a kind of authenticity often missing in mainstream records. Artists like Johnny Cash, Bon Iver, Sufjan Stevens, and even modern storytellers like Phoebe Bridgers have cited Nebraska as an influence. The album taught a generation that less can be more—that truth doesn't need a backing band.

But beyond its musical influence, Nebraska matters because it was a brave decision. Springsteen was at the height of his fame and could have easily followed the formula that had already made him a star. Instead, he chose the harder path—a quiet, stripped-down record that exposed his internal struggles, moral doubts, and fears.

That vulnerability is why Nebraska endures. It showed that even "The Boss" was still just a man trying to make sense of the world. Springsteen himself has acknowledged that Nebraska wasn't meant to be a commercial success; it was meant to be honest. And that honesty—its quiet intensity, its refusal to bend—is what continues to draw in listeners old and new.

Springsteen's Continued Influence on Music and Film

Bruce Springsteen's influence on music is well documented, but Nebraska and the spirit behind it have shaped more than just albums. They have seeped into visual storytelling, character development, and the emotional tone of modern cinema.

Springsteen's songs have always carried a narrative weight—miniature films in themselves, complete with characters, settings, arcs, and resolutions. Nebraska, in particular, shifted the tone from wide-screen rock to something closer to indie cinema. The album's aesthetic—quiet, stark, unsettling—has influenced a generation of filmmakers exploring American identity, small-town decay, and moral ambiguity.

Directors like the Coen Brothers, David Gordon Green, Jeff Nichols, and even Terrence Malick have made films that echo the emotional texture of Nebraska. The upcoming film Deliver Me from Nowhere takes this influence full circle. Directed by Scott Cooper and starring Jeremy Allen White as Springsteen, the film chronicles the deeply personal and creatively charged period leading to the creation of Nebraska.

Rather than sensationalizing the rockstar lifestyle, it focuses on the stillness, the doubt, and the isolation that fueled Springsteen's most haunting work. In portraying this quiet phase of his life, the film dares to slow things down. There are no pyrotechnics, no arena tours, and no chart-topping singles—just a man alone with his past and a recorder.

And that's what makes the story powerful. It aligns with what modern audiences increasingly seek: depth over dazzle, introspection over noise. Moreover, Springsteen's broader influence on film can be felt in how characters are written. His songs often feature everyday people pushed to moral edges: factory workers, criminals, single parents, drifters, and dreamers.

These are the same people who populate some of the most compelling dramas in contemporary cinema and television. His ability to see dignity in struggle has made its way into countless scripts, where the extraordinary is found in the ordinary. In music, Springsteen continues to serve as a reference point for authenticity.

In an era where digital perfection is the norm, his approach—especially during the Nebraska era—offers a compelling counterpoint. New artists cite him not just for his sound but for his discipline, honesty, and work ethic. Albums like Nebraska serve as case studies in the power of restraint, reminding songwriters that the message should never be lost in the mix.

To this day, Springsteen is still performing, still writing, and still evolving. But Nebraska remains a defining chapter. It's the album that proved success doesn't have to shout. Sometimes it just needs to tell the truth. And in a cultural moment craving that truth, both the album and the film that honors its creation feel more essential than ever.

Together, Nebraska and Deliver Me from Nowhere represent not just a moment in music history, but a lasting reminder that vulnerability, simplicity, and depth never go out of style. They invite us to listen more closely—not just to the music, but to ourselves. And that might be Springsteen's greatest legacy of all.

Printed in Dunstable, United Kingdom